The Common Core Readiness Guide to Reading™

TIPS & TRICKS FOR ANALYZING IDEAS, EVENTS, AND INDIVIDUALS

Sandra K. Athans and Robin W. Parente

ROSEN
PUBLISHING®

New York

Published in 2015 by The Rosen Publishing Group, Inc.
29 East 21st Street, New York, NY 10010

Copyright © 2015 by The Rosen Publishing Group, Inc.
First Edition

Library of Congress Cataloging-in-Publication Data

Athans, Sandra K., 1958–
Tips & tricks for analyzing ideas, events, and individuals/Sandra K. Athans and Robin W. Parente. — First Edition.
     pages cm. — (The Common Core Readiness Guide to Reading)
Audience: Grades 5–8.
Includes bibliographical references and index.
ISBN 978-1-4777-7531-8 (library bound) — ISBN 978-1-4777-7533-2 (pbk.) — ISBN 978-1-4777-7534-9 (6-pack)
1. Reading comprehension—Study and teaching (Middle school) 2. Critical thinking in children—Study and teaching (Middle school) 3. Reader-response criticism—Study and teaching (Middle school) 4. Reading—Language experience approach. I. Parente, Robin W. II. Title. III. Title: Tips and tricks for analyzing ideas, events, and individuals.
LB1573.7.A87 2014
428.4071'2—dc23

                                                                    2013049990

Manufactured in the United States of America

Contents

Introduction

The Common Core Reading Standards are a set of skills designed to prepare you for entering college or beginning your career. They're grouped into broad College and Career Ready Anchor Standards, and they help you use reasoning and evidence in ways that will serve you well now and in the future.

The skills build from kindergarten to the twelfth grade. Grades six through eight take the spotlight here. You may already have noticed changes in your classrooms that are based on the standards—deeper-level reading, shorter passages, an emphasis on informational texts, or an overall increase in rigor within your daily activities.

This book will help you understand, practice, and independently apply the skills through easy-to-use "tips and tricks." Gaining mastery of the skills is the goal.

Your teachers may use close reading for some of their instruction. During close reading, you read shorter passages more deeply and analytically.

The Common Core standards are designed to be relevant to the real world and reflect the knowledge and skills young people will need for success in college and careers.

Close-reading passages often have rich, complex content. They contain grade-level vocabulary words, sentence structures, and literary techniques. Reading a short, three-page passage closely could take two to three days or more. The benefit to you is that you get a deeper, more valuable understanding of what you've read. Close reading is a critical part of the new Common Core Reading Standards and is used throughout this book.

Other well-known reading comprehension skills remain valuable. Visualizing, asking questions, synthesizing, and other traditional strategies work well together with the Common Core skills covered here.

This book focuses on Anchor Standard 3: analyzing ideas, events, and individuals over the course of a text. In the next chapter, we'll break these skills apart and look at them closely. Also, the tips and tricks that can help you gain mastery of this standard are introduced. Some feature visual icons that will be used throughout this book.

In the passages that follow, you tag along with "Expert Readers" as they think aloud while close reading from different passages of literature (fiction) and informational text (nonfiction). Visual icons that represent the tips and tricks appear in the margins and prompt the Expert Reader. Ways in which the Expert Reader applies them appear in "Expert Reader" margin notes. You'll also review multiple-choice and written response questions completed by the Experts. Explanations that support their reasoning are provided.

After you gain an understanding of how the skill is applied, it's your turn to try with guided practice. You'll apply the skill independently and perform a self-evaluation by checking your responses against answers provided. Based on your responses, you can determine if another pass through the Expert Reader's examples might be helpful—or if you've mastered the skill.

CHAPTER 1

A QUICK AND EASY OVERVIEW: THE SKILLS AND THE TIPS AND TRICKS

Let's examine the skills involved with analyzing ideas, events, and individuals closely so that we understand them. We know that the word "analyze" is a verb, so it's something we actively do. When you analyze while reading, you carefully examine, inspect, and consider the text in order to fully understand it. As you analyze text, you must rely on its content—not on knowledge you gained elsewhere. Sometimes you may have to break text down into smaller, more manageable units, such as sentences or paragraphs, in order to understand it more fully.

You may also need to make inferences about ideas or events not explicitly stated. An inference is a conclusion you make by interpreting clues provided in the passage—it's as if you're reading between the lines. Your inferences must be reasonably based on something concrete in the text.

In this standard, you will be looking specifically at the development of ideas, events, and individuals or characters as they are presented throughout the course of the passage. At times this may involve taking a close look at a character's dialogue or the anecdotes

Jump-start clues help a reader to engage with the text. Visual clues spark ideas that are molded and reshaped continuously.

analyzing the way in which these components interact is another avenue that we will consider while building our knowledge and skill with this standard.

These skills are useful when reading literature and informational text, and when reading within history/social studies, science, and technical subjects. They're also useful for many of your daily, real-life activities. As you will see, there are mild nuances in the manner in which you apply these skills to the different genres. Yet with practice, these adjustments become automatic.

As you progress in grade levels, you're expected to analyze the components of individuals, events, and ideas more deeply, as well as more broadly in terms of the ways in which they interact with each other.

Analysis Tips & Tricks

Text Analysis: There are several easy-to-use tips and tricks that can help you analyze the individuals, events, and ideas within reading passages. Some are useful as you begin to read, while others guide you throughout your reading. Here's a quick overview of them. The icons featured below are used in subsequent chapters to show you how the tips and tricks are used in action with literature and informational texts.

● **Launching "Jump-Start" Clues:** Before you dive into reading a piece of text, scan it quickly. Notice and take a visual inventory of everything you see. The title, subheadings, boldface print, and other features like photographs or charts will give you valuable clues about the content and genre. Authors select and use text features purposefully. It's often helpful to ask yourself: *What could the title mean or what purpose do the special features serve?*

● **Using Genre and Text Structure (Flexibly) to Build and Check Understanding:** You already know a lot about the different genres and their structures. For example, in works of fiction, characters and a setting are introduced, a problem is identified, and events lead to a solution or improvement. With informational text, authors organize ideas in cause and effect or other structures that help readers grasp and remember important information. Working with these structures to guide and validate your understanding and analysis is helpful. You might ask yourself: *Does the story unfold in a way that makes sense, or does the information seem valid and cohesive?*

● **Breaking Apart Literary Elements:** In works of literature, breaking apart and analyzing the literary elements separately is often helpful. The characters, events, and setting of a story are among the literary elements that an author carefully crafts together to move the plot forward. Determining how these elements develop and interact within the passage helps us build richer, more meaningful understandings of the story. Also, we may begin to gain an appreciation for an author's style. As you're reading, keep in mind the following:

Character: What are the characters saying, doing, thinking, and feeling? Does their dialogue or actions give us insight into the story?

Events: What is happening and why? How are events unfolding? Are they predictable or not?

Setting: How important is the setting? In what ways does it contribute to the story?

Interaction: How do the characters, events, and setting come together?

Quick Check Self-Evaluation for Analyzing Ideas, Events, and Individuals

Determining how well you've mastered the tips and tricks for analyzing ideas, events, and individuals is important. One way to do this is by gauging your success with the following tasks:

√ I can summarize the passage.

√ My summary is cohesive and makes sense based on evidence.

√ I can identify key ideas and the author's message.

√ My ideas can be supported using specific examples from the text.

Elements found within informational text can also be broken apart for analysis. Here, authors may use examples or anecdotes to impart information. Likewise, they may use comparisons, analogies, or other methods of categorization to establish connections among and distinctions between individuals, events, and ideas. Considering how an author has launched and developed information is key.

Also keep in mind that authors of informational text have a point to make about a topic. They frequently want to change your thinking in some way or add to your understanding and will sometimes use an expository, procedural, or persuasive text structure. Awareness of these structures helps a reader analyze ideas, events, and individuals and improves comprehension.

It may be necessary for you to use evidence-based inferencing—or reading between the lines—to explain actions, events, or ideas that are not explicitly stated in literature and informational passages.

● **Consider the Tone of the Story or Passage:** An author creates the tone or mood of a passage purposefully. Words, phrases, and descriptive interactions among individuals or characters, events, and ideas help establish tone; how an author chooses to express something sets the tone. Recognizing the tone can help you with your analysis. Some questions you might consider while monitoring tone are: *How are you affected by what you have read? How does the author influence your emotional engagement with the passage?*

● **Tune in to Your Inside Voice:** Your mind is actively making sense as you read. Listening to your thoughts or your mind's dialogue helps you grasp meaning. Connecting new ideas to known ideas is the way your mind builds cohesive meaning. Monitoring your thoughts, including your questions, is critical. *Do characters' motives, events in the story, and/or ideas seem unusual or out of place? How do charts, tables, or other special features included within a passage build your understanding? Are your reactions likely what the author intended?* Authors often build reader engagement by posing questions. However, it's also important for you to distinguish when you're confused and need to implement fix-up strategies like rereading.

● **Avoid Common Pitfalls:** Sometimes we can become distracted by something in the text, which could steer us away from an author's intended meaning. Staying engaged and focused while ensuring that your ideas square with text-based evidence is critical. It's sometimes helpful to validate your interpretation by considering your answer to the following question: *I know this because...*Your answer to this question must be found within the passage.

Analyzing ideas, events, and individuals in a work of fiction helps readers construct an understanding that aligns with an author's intended meaning.

As you practice and gain skill with these tips and tricks, you'll find that they work together and often become indistinguishable. This is a sure sign that they've become authentic and automatic and kick in when and where they're needed.

CHAPTER 2

ANALYZING IDEAS, EVENTS, AND INDIVIDUALS IN LITERATURE: EXPERT READER MODEL

Let's see how to apply the tips and tricks to literature. Remember literature could be adventure stories, historical fiction, mysteries, myths, science fiction, realistic fiction, allegories, parodies, and more.

Literature often features elements such as characters, problems or conflicts, a setting and plot, events and episodes, and a problem resolution. Authors weave these elements together carefully, mindful that they interact in meaningful and engaging ways. Looking closely at these elements and their interaction gives us a richer understanding of the story. It is also more likely that our understanding is more in keeping with the author's intention.

Specific genres within literature also have specific characteristics and features. For example, science fiction often examines imaginary scientifc progress of the future, while realistic fiction and historical fiction include characters that are believable and events or episodes that could happen or might have happened in the past. Your ability to analyze elements of literature relies on your grade-level knowledge of literature basics.

Plan of Action

The passage in this chapter is an adaptation of a chapter appearing in *My Antonia* by Willa Cather. You'll be reading the passage and following as an Expert Reader thinks through a sampling of the tips and tricks in the margin notes. (Review the icon descriptors in chapter 1 for reference.) It's as if you're tagging along with the Expert Reader.

You'll also observe the Expert Reader perform a self-evaluation by sharing a summary and the thinking behind it. Then, tag along as the Expert Reader tackles some multiple-choice and constructed response questions and demonstrates how to analyze ideas, events, and individuals in literature.

Willa Sibert Cather (1873–1947) was an acclaimed American author recognized for her novels that depict frontier life on the Great Plains.

After this, it's your turn to practice. In chapter 3, you'll be reading a passage where guided practice prompts cue your use of the tips and tricks for literature. You can check your thinking against provided possible responses.

🕮 EXPERT READER:

This passage is a chapter that has been adapted from a book-length work. The names Shimerda and Antonia could suggest that the story may have a regional setting. The Reader's Note may give me more information.

The Reader's Note helps to clarify my ideas. Some characters are from Bohemia, which is outside of the United States, while the setting is Black Hawk, Nebraska. I suspect the genre is realistic fiction or historical fiction. I'll monitor my ideas.

The story is told from Jim's point of view, and the problem seems to be that he doesn't like how Antonia treats him. He is pleased that events cause her to consider him an equal.

Adapted from:

My Antonia 🏃

By Willa Cather

(**Note to the Reader:** *After his parents died, Jim Burdon went to live with his grandparents in Black Hawk, Nebraska. While traveling there aboard a train, he met Antonia Shimerda. She and her family are immigrants from Bohemia. They, too, settle in Black Hawk.*)

Much as I liked Antonia, I hated a superior tone that she sometimes took with me. She was four years older than I and had seen more of the world; but I was a boy and she was a girl, and I resented her protecting manner. Before the autumn was over, she began to treat me more like an equal and to defer to me in other things than reading lessons. This change came about from an adventure we had together.

One day when I rode over to the Shimerdas', I found Antonia starting off on foot for Russian Peter's house, to borrow a spade her brother Ambrosch needed. I offered to take her on the pony, and she got up behind me. We found Russian Peter digging his potatoes. As we rode away with the spade, Antonia suggested that we stop at the prairie-dog-town and dig into one of the holes. We could find out whether they ran straight down, or were horizontal, like mole-holes.

The dog-town was spread out over ten acres. I tied Dude down in a draw, and we went wandering about, looking for a hole that would be easy to dig. We were examining a big hole with two entrances. I was walking backward, in a crouching position, when I heard Antonia scream. She was standing opposite me, pointing behind me and shouting something in Bohemian. I whirled round, and there was the biggest snake I had ever seen. He was sunning himself, lying in long loose waves, like a letter "W." He twitched and began to coil slowly. He was not merely a big snake—he was a circus monstrosity. His abominable muscularity, his loathsome, fluid motion, somehow made me sick. He was as thick as my leg, and looked as if millstones couldn't crush him. He lifted his hideous little head and rattled. I didn't run because I didn't think of it. I felt cornered and couldn't move. I saw his coils tighten—now he would spring, spring his length. I ran up and drove at his head with my spade, struck him fairly across the neck, and in a minute he was about my feet in wavy loops. Antonia ran up behind me. Even after I had pounded his ugly head flat, his body kept on coiling and winding, doubling and falling back on itself. I walked away and turned my back. I felt seasick.

Antonia came after me, crying, "O Jimmy, he not bite you? You sure? Why you not run when I say?"

EXPERT READER:

The episodes in the snake adventure unfold quickly and vividly through Jim's retelling. Some details seem exaggerated. Although some of the vocabulary words are tricky, I get the gist that the snake is huge and frightening. I'll reread this to study it more deeply.

"What did you jabber Bohunk for? You might have told me there was a snake behind me!" I said, impatiently.

"I know I am just awful, Jim, I was so scared." She took my handkerchief from my pocket and tried to wipe my face with it, but I snatched it away from her. I suppose I looked as sick as I felt. I never know you was so brave, Jim," she went on comfortingly. "You is just like big mans; you wait for him lift his head and then you go for him. Ain't you feel scared a bit? Now we take that snake home and show everybody. Nobody ain't seen in this kawntree so big snake like you kill."

She went on in this strain until I began to think that I had longed for this opportunity, and had hailed it with joy. Cautiously we went back to the snake; I took a long piece of string from my pocket, and Antonia lifted his head with the spade while I tied a noose around it. We pulled him out straight and measured him; he was about five and a half feet long. I began to feel proud of him, to have a kind of respect for his age and size. When we dragged him down into the draw, Dude sprang off to the end of his tether and shivered all over—wouldn't let us come near him.

We decided that Antonia should ride Dude home, and I would walk. As she rode along slowly, she kept shouting back to me about how

EXPERT READER:

Jim is harsh with Antonia. He lashes out, calling her "jabber Bohunk" and is angered by her inability to warn him. He even pushes her away when she tries to wipe his face. The emotionally charged tone seems to suggest a turning point in the story.

Speaking in broken English, Antonia tells Jim very openly how she views him as a man as a result of his bravery. Her dialogue also implies that she is proud of him and is eager to show off the dead snake.

astonished everybody would be. I followed with the spade over my shoulder, dragging my snake. The great land had never looked to me so big and free. If the red grass were full of rattlers, I was equal to them all. ⊬ Nevertheless, I stole furtive glances behind me now and then to see that no avenging mate, older and bigger, was racing up from the rear.

The sun had set when we reached the house. Otto Fuchs was the first one we met. Antonia called him to come quick and look. He did not say anything for a minute, but scratched his head and turned the snake over with his boot.

"Where did you run onto that beauty, Jim?"

"Up at the dog-town," I answered.

"Kill him yourself? He could stand right up and talk to you, he could. Did he fight hard?"

Antonia broke in: "He fight something awful! He is all over Jimmy's boots. I scream for him to run, but he just hit and hit that snake like he was crazy."

Otto winked at me. After Antonia rode on he said: "Got him in the head first crack, didn't you? That was just as well."

We hung him up to the windmill and when I went down to the

EXPERT READER:

⊬ Jim's character also seems to change as a result of the snake adventure. I also see that he thinks he's "equal" to the rattlers, a word he uses earlier in the passage to describe how he wants to be treated by Antonia.

EXPERT READER:

This exchange between Otto, Antonia, and Jim is interesting. Antonia exaggerates Jim's battle with the snake, and Otto winks at Jim as if he understands this. Maybe Otto's character is introduced here to show a deeper connection is building between the other two characters? I get the gist of what's happening, but I'll reread this section to better shape my ideas.

EXPERT READER:

The problem introduced at the beginning of the story seems to be resolved. I also think Jim begins to understand his own feelings about Antonia.

kitchen, I found Antonia standing in the middle of the floor, telling the story with a great deal of color.

That snake hung on our corral fence for several days; some of the neighbors came to see it and agreed that it was the biggest rattler ever killed in those parts. She liked me better from that time on, and she never took an arrogant air with me again. I had killed a big snake—I was now a big fellow.

Quick Check Self-Evaluation for Analyzing Ideas, Events, and Individuals

Let's take a break here to let the Expert Reader summarize and analyze this passage:

In this passage, the main character, Jim, complains about the condescending and childlike way his neighbor, Antonia, treated him and then recounts how an unplanned adventure changed their relationship. As he and Antonia were exploring prairie dog holes in the grasslands of Black Hawk, Nebraska, he unexpectedly disturbed a massive, 5.5 foot [1.7 m] long rattler snake. Immobile with fear, he manages to kill the snake with a shovel just as it rose its head to strike. Afterward, Antonia admits to her fear and her inability to help and sees Jim as a "big mans" and flaunts his bravery. Jim, too, recognizes something new about himself—that he is equal to other things around him. Through Jim's story, the author shares a very believable story of two kids who grow and change as they learn about themselves, their relationship to others, and their place in the larger world.

The fictional town of Black Hawk, Nebraska, is based on the actual town of Red Cloud, Nebraska, where Willa Cather grew up. The grassy landscape there is home to prairie dogs that live in colonies or "towns" burrowed beneath the ground.

Expert Reader: I'm satisfied with this summary. I thought about the passage carefully, I reread sections to check my understanding against text evidence, and I used key examples to support my ideas. I'm ready to challenge my thinking by answering multiple-choice and constructed response questions. Notice that in some cases, more than one answer could be considered correct. It is important to use evidence to build a case for the best answer. Carefully reviewing evidence by returning to the passage will be helpful. Then gauging which response is best supported through the evidence is critical.

Mini Assessment

1. Reread this sentence from the story: "You wait for him lift his head and then you go for him. Ain't you feel scared a bit?" What does the dialogue suggest about Antonia's interpretation of events?

a) She thought Jim waited too long to kill the snake.

b) She believed Jim's fears interfered with his planned method of killing the snake.

c) She believes Jim's method of killing the snake was carefully planned and carried out fearlessly.

d) She thought Jim was lucky to have killed the snake.

2. Although Jim concludes that Antonia "liked him better" and never "took an arrogant air" with him again, how has Jim changed from the beginning to the end of the story?

a) He becomes more comfortable with the Nebraska prairie.

b) He recognizes his limits and fears in new ways.

c) He becomes less critical of Antonia.

d) He recognizes his own greater capabilities.

3. Reread this sentence from the story: "Otto winked at me. After Antonia rode on he said: 'Got him in the head first crack, didn't you? That was just as well, Jim.'" Why does he respond in this manner to Jim?

a) To show he thought Jim had other reasons to dramatize how he killed the snake.

b) To show Jim he was lucky he killed the snake with the first crack.

c) To secretly share the knowledge with Jim that killing an older snake was not difficult.

d) To show Jim he performed well killing the snake.

Check your answers. Were you correct?

1. c) is the correct answer. Antonia has mistaken Jim's fear and hesitation as a carefully timed plan. Also, she cannot believe he was unafraid, even "a bit" and asks him about this. The other answers do not reflect her interpretation of the event.

2. d) is the correct answer. Jim soon becomes proud of killing the snake, he feels equal to any rattlers that may be lurking nearby, and thinks about the land and how it looked big and free. These ideas support and reflect his feelings about himself.

3. a) is the correct answer. Otto's wink suggests that he shares a secret or unspoken ideas with Jim. Taken together with his comment that he recognized Jim killed the snake with his first hit, Otto implies that Antonia's boasting may have been cause for Jim's actions.

Expert Reader: I'm satisfied with my responses. In all cases, I returned to the text to check against evidence. Sometimes the evidence was right there—explicit in a character's actions or words. Other times, I had to dig a little deeper and use clues and inferences. In either case, my answers square with the evidence. Now I feel I'm ready to try a constructed response question.

Question: Jim claims the snake adventure brought about a change in Antonia's attitude toward him—how she began to treat him like "an equal" and defer to him for "other things than reading." In what other ways is the event of the snake encounter important to the story? How does it shape the characters and plot of the chapter? Use details to support your answers.

Possible response: The snake encounter is important to the story as it explains why Antonia's attitude about Jim changes. This is the main reason why Jim, who is the narrator, chooses to tell it. However, the story also serves a greater purpose: It lets us see into each character, teaches us more about them, and it shows us how Jim changes along with Antonia. The snake scene is fast-paced and charged with emotion that causes both characters to act unpredictably. Antonia is scared and cries a warning to Jim in a language that he cannot understand. She is unable to protect him. Jim overcomes his fears at the last moment and swings at the snake and kills it. The event pushes both characters and challenges them to respond to a new situation in new ways. Antonia was no longer the protector, and Jim clearly did not need her protection. The plot of the chapter shows how their relationship changed as a result of their own changes.

Conclusion

How well have you grasped the Expert Reader's use of the tips and tricks to analyze ideas, events, and individuals? Decide if you're ready to move on to the guided practice in the next chapter or if you would like to take another pass through the Expert Reader's model.

CHAPTER 3

ANALYZING IDEAS, EVENTS, AND INDIVIDUALS IN LITERATURE: GUIDED PRACTICE

Now it's time for you to apply the tips and tricks during your close reading of a passage. The practice prompt icons will guide you (review chapter 1 for icon descriptors). Check to see if your responses to the prompts match possible responses provided.

An Adaptation from: *Call of the Wild*: Chapter 1 "Into the Primitive"
By Jack London

Buck did not read the newspapers, or he would have known that trouble was brewing, not for himself, but for every strong, long-haired dog, from Puget Sound to San Diego. Because men, groping in the Arctic darkness, had found gold, thousands of men were

📺 GUIDED PRACTICE PROMPT:

What jump-start clues do you notice? Possible response: This passage is an adapted chapter from a book-length work. The book's title suggests a wilderness setting or event, and the chapter title suggests an old or ancient time period. I'll monitor these ideas.

What are you thinking? Possible response: Although the first sentence could be misleading, I suspect Buck might be a dog.

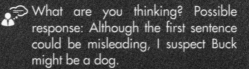

GUIDED PRACTICE PROMPT:

What do you notice about the genre and text structure? Possible response: I suspect Buck, a dog, is the main character and this is a fictional story. I also think the problem is introduced here. Buck may encounter trouble as a result of the gold rush.

rushing into the Northland. These men wanted dogs, and the dogs they wanted were heavy dogs, with strong muscles by which to toil, and furry coats to protect them from the frost.

Buck lived at a big house in the sun-kissed Santa Clara Valley. Judge Miller's place, it was called. It stood back from the road, half hidden among the trees. There were great stables, where a dozen grooms and boys lived, rows of vine-clad servants' cottages, green pastures, orchards, and berry patches. Then there was the big cement tank where Judge Miller's boys took their morning plunge and kept cool in the hot afternoon.

Over this great kingdom Buck ruled. Here he was born, and here he had lived the four years of his life. Buck was neither house-dog nor kennel-dog. The whole realm was his. He plunged into the swimming tank or went hunting with the Judge's sons; he escorted the Judge's daughters on long twilight or early morning rambles; on wintry nights he lay at the Judge's feet before the roaring library fire; and he carried the Judge's grandsons on his back. He was king—king over all creeping, crawling, flying things of Judge Miller's place, humans included.

Buck's father was a huge St. Bernard and had been the Judge's inseparable companion. Buck hoped to follow in the way of his father. He was not so large, though, and

GUIDED PRACTICE PROMPT:

How can a breakdown of literary elements help here? Possible response: The description of the setting of Buck's home features a lot of visual details. I get a good idea of Buck's comfortable life.

weighed only one hundred and forty pounds. This is probably because his mother had been a shepherd dog. Nevertheless, with his one hundred and forty pounds, he carried himself in royal fashion. This was the manner of Buck in the fall of 1897, when the Klondike gold strike dragged men from all over the world into the frozen North. But Buck did not read the newspapers, and he did not know that Manuel, one of the gardener's helpers, was in need of money. While the Judge was at a meeting of the Raisin Growers' Association, and the boys were busy organizing an athletic club, no one saw Manuel lead Buck off through the orchard on what Buck imagined was merely a stroll. And except for a stranger already in waiting there, no one saw them arrive at the train station. This man talked with Manuel, and money was exchanged between them.

"You might wrap up the goods before you deliver 'm," the stranger said gruffly, and Manuel doubled a piece of rope around Buck's neck under the collar.

"Twist it, an' you'll choke 'm," said Manuel. Buck had accepted the rope with quiet dignity. He had learned to trust in men he knew, and to give them credit for a wisdom that outreached his own. But when the ends of the rope were placed in the stranger's hands, he growled.

GUIDED PRACTICE PROMPT:

How does the tone of the passage help build your understanding? Possible response: The tone shifts. It is lulling as I learn about Buck's home and activities. Then, I get frightened for him when I learn of Manuel's need for money.

GUIDED PRACTICE PROMPT:

How can a breakdown of literary elements help here? Possible response: The stranger's character is unlikable. He treats Buck as "goods" and speaks gruffly. Meanwhile, Buck's character is so likeable. I'm concerned for Buck.

What are you thinking? Possible response: Buck's quiet dignity and trust are going to get him into trouble.

But to his surprise the rope tightened around his neck, shutting off his breath. In quick rage he sprang at the man; but the man grabbed him by the throat, and threw him over on his back. Buck struggled in a fury, his tongue lolling out of his mouth and his great chest panting. Never in all his life had he been treated so poorly. And never in all his life had he been so angry. As his strength gave out, his eyes glazed, and he fell unconscious. He knew nothing when the train stopped and the two men threw him into the baggage car. ⟋

The next he knew, the hoarse shriek of a locomotive whistling told him where he was. He had travelled too often with the Judge not to know the sensation of riding in a baggage car. He opened his eyes, and into them came the unbridled anger of a kidnapped king. Buck attempted to face and challenge his tormentors, but he was thrown down again and then flung into a cage-like crate.

Several times during the night whenever a door opened, he sprang to his feet expecting to see the Judge, or the boys at least. But they did not come. ⟋ In the morning four men entered and picked up the crate. More tormentors, Buck decided, for they were evil looking, ragged and unkempt. He stormed and raged at them through the bars. They only laughed and poked sticks

GUIDED PRACTICE PROMPT:

⟋ How can a breakdown of literary elements help here? Possible response: The narrator makes us aware of Buck's thoughts. From this, we can easily see the contrast between the life Buck had with the Judge and the events that are unfolding now.

GUIDED PRACTICE PROMPT:

⟋ How can a breakdown of literary elements help here? Possible response: I'm thinking that Buck is not going to be able to escape the inevitable—the problem, setting, and the immediate events are woven together and leading me to think that Buck will end up in the North with the gold miners.

at him, which he attacked with his teeth till he realized that that was what they wanted. So instead, he lay down quietly and allowed the crate to be lifted into a wagon. Then he, and the crate, began a passage through many hands. Clerks in the express office took charge of him; he was carted about in another wagon; a truck carried him, with an assortment of boxes and parcels, upon a ferry steamer; he was trucked off the steamer into a great railway depot, and finally he was placed in an express train where he remained for two days and nights without eating or drinking. His eyes turned blood-shot, and he was changed into a raging animal. Even the Judge would not have recognized him. 👤💬

GUIDED PRACTICE PROMPT:

👤💬 What are you thinking? Possible response: Buck has undergone a big transformation in this first chapter. Although he was surprised by his mistreatment, he is quickly making sense of his new environment. Although I'm fearful for him, I'm also hopeful.

Quick Check Self-Evaluation for Analyzing Ideas, Events, and Individuals

At this point, you should be able to summarize the story and think about the meaning the author intended you to get (Refer to page 11 to review the criteria). What is the strongest evidence that may lead you to the author's message? Go ahead and try it! Talk it through or get a piece of paper and write it down. (See the Expert Reader's summary.) Once you're satisfied and have checked your response, challenge your thinking and answer the multiple-choice and constructed response questions that follow.

Expert Reader: This chapter introduces the main character of this story, Buck, a dog that has spent his life enjoying the kingdomlike grounds of his owner, Judge Miller, and his family. Buck is unaware of the trouble that surrounds him and is unsuspectingly kidnapped away from his comfortable home. He is mistreated during his kidnapping and while he is transported to a place far from his home. Buck is angry and feels threatened by his kidnapers, whom he calls tormentors. Although at first he fights back against them, he soon realizes he is better off accepting his captivity.

(Your summary may be somewhat different from the Expert Reader's, and that's OK, as long as it holds up under scrutiny and squares with the supporting text evidence.)

Mini Assessment

1. Reread this dialogue from the story: "Twist it, an' you'll choke 'm," said Manuel. What is Manuel's motive for saying this to the stranger?

   a) Manuel regretted that he had to exchange Buck for money.

   b) Manuel cautioned the stranger not to twist the rope.

   c) Manuel knew Buck was strong and would need to be controlled.

   d) Manuel wasn't prepared for the exchange.

2. Reread these sentences from the story: "Buck had accepted the rope with quiet dignity. He had learned to trust in men he knew, and to give them credit for a wisdom that outreached his own." What do these lines reveal about Buck and how does this move the story plot forward?

   a) It explains why Buck misjudged the events that led to his captivity.

   b) It explains why Buck lay quietly in his crate instead of fending off his tormentors.

   c) It explains why Buck trusted that the Judge and his family would come to his rescue.

   d) It explains that Buck had a dignified upbringing.

3. Buck misjudges many of the hazards around him. Which lines from the story best reveal that Buck eventually recognizes the kind of danger he is in?

a) "He opened his eyes, and into them came the unbridled anger of a kidnapped king."

b) "But when the ends of the rope were placed in the stranger's hands, he growled."

c) "Buck struggled in a fury, his tongue lolling out of his mouth and his great chest panting."

d) "But Buck did not read the newspapers, and he did not know that Manuel, one of the gardener's helpers, was in need of money."

Check your answers. Were you correct?

1. c) is the correct answer. Although we don't know much about Manuel, we understand a lot about his character through his heartless betrayal of Buck. Manuel knew Buck would fight for his freedom and need to be controlled.

2. a) is the correct answer. Buck misjudged the events that led to his captivity. He allowed the rope to be placed around his neck because of his trust in human wisdom. Choice b) happened sometime after Buck was held captive, and choices c) and d) are inaccurate.

3. a) is the correct answer. This episode follows the others in choices b) through c) and shows that Buck recognizes his kinglike lifestyle is threatened.

What do you think so far? Is your understanding and analysis of the ideas, events, and characters taking shape? Did you return to the passage and find evidence to support your responses? Did your answers square with the evidence? Are you comfortable discussing or writing a response to the following constructed response question?

The character Buck in Jack London's *Call of the Wild* is based on a real dog, a mixed St. Bernard-Scotch Collie, that belonged to a friend of the author.

Question: How does the author build and develop Buck's character? How does Buck's character shape the plot?

Possible response: From the moment Buck's character is introduced, he surprises us. First, we learn that he is out of touch with the trouble brewing around him because he doesn't read newspapers. It is only after this that we learn the reason why—Buck is a dog! We come to know much about Buck through the narrator, who tells us mostly about Buck's life with the Judge. In that life, Buck is compared to a king reigning over a kingdom. He roams freely and is in charge of all things. It is within this setting that Buck develops his character; he trusts humans and believes in their wisdom, and his only goal is to become a favored companion. When Buck is suddenly kidnapped from this environment and is tormented by his captors, he lashes out in anger. As this only gets him into more trouble, he begins to trust his instinct and judgment and accepts his captivity. Now that his environment has changed, Buck must change. Figuring out how to survive in a new, unknown world seems to launch the plot of this story.

Conclusion

How well have you grasped the tips and tricks to analyze ideas, events, and individuals in literature? Based on your performance and self-evaluation, decide if you're ready to move to the next chapter or if you would like to take another pass through this guided practice.

CHAPTER 4

ANALYZING IDEAS, EVENTS, AND INDIVIDUALS IN INFORMATIONAL TEXT: EXPERT READER MODEL

Now let's see how to apply the tips and tricks to informational text. Remember, informational text is a type of nonfiction, or factual, text that is written to inform the reader, explain something, or convey information about the natural and social worlds. Informational text can include newspaper and magazine articles; essays; speeches; opinion pieces; editorials; and historical, scientific, technical or economic accounts.

Authors of informational text have a point to make about a topic. They frequently want to change your thinking in some way or add to your understanding and will sometimes use an expository, procedural, or persuasive text structure. Awareness of these structures helps a reader analyze ideas, events, and individuals and improves comprehension.

Plan of Action

The passage in this chapter is an excerpt from a speech given by

Abraham Lincoln is considered one of the United States' greatest presidents. He is known for preserving the Union of the United States and for being instrumental in the passage of the Thirteenth Amendment to the Constitution, which outlawed slavery.

reading the excerpt and following as an Expert Reader thinks through the tips and tricks—this time as they are applied to informational text. You may want to refresh your memory by reviewing the tips and tricks before beginning.

Again, you'll observe the Expert Reader perform a self-evaluation through the sharing of a summary and the thinking behind it. Finally, you'll tag along while the Expert Reader works through some multiple-choice questions and a constructed response question to get the full impact of how to analyze ideas, events, and individuals in informational text.

Then, in the chapter that follows, it will be your turn to practice. You'll start by reading a speech where guided practice prompts and icons cue your use of the tips and tricks. You can check your thinking against the provided possible responses.

🏃 An Excerpt from:
Abraham Lincoln's Annual Message to Congress,
December 1, 1862

(Lincoln was elected the sixteenth president of the United States in November 1860. South Carolina immediately voted to secede, or leave, the Union. Mississippi, Florida, Alabama, Georgia, Louisiana, Texas, Virginia, Arkansas, Tennessee, and North Carolina soon followed. In April of 1861, Lincoln declared a state of insurrection and called for volunteers to enlist in the Union Army. By December 1862, Union and Confederate forces had been fighting each other for over one and a half years.)

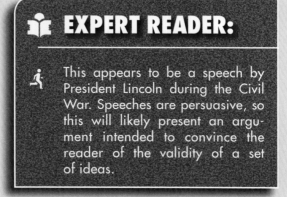

📖 EXPERT READER:

🏃 This appears to be a speech by President Lincoln during the Civil War. Speeches are persuasive, so this will likely present an argument intended to convince the reader of the validity of a set of ideas.

There is no line, straight or crooked, suitable for a national boundary. Trace through from east to west upon the line between the free and the slave country, and we shall find a little more than one-third of its length are rivers, easy to be crossed, and populated, while nearly all its remaining length are merely surveyors' lines, over which people may walk back and forth without any consciousness of their presence. No part of this line can be made any more difficult to pass, by writing it down on paper or parchment as a national boundary. ⅄ The fact of separation, if it comes, gives up, on the part of the seceding section, the fugitive-slave clause, along with all other constitutional obligations upon the section seceded from, while I should expect no treaty stipulation would be ever made to take its place. 📖

But there is another difficulty. The great interior region bounded east by the Alleghenies, north by the British dominions, west by the Rocky Mountains, and south by the line along which the culture of corn and cotton meets... already has above ten millions of people, and will have fifty millions within fifty years, if not prevented by any political folly or mistake. It contains more than one-third of the country owned by the United States—certainly more than one million of square miles. A glance at the map shows that, territorially speaking, it is the great body of the republic. The other parts are but marginal borders to it, the magnificent

EXPERT READER:

Speeches are structured by logically organizing reasons for a belief, attitude, or proposed action. I'll need to gather information and recognize the points Lincoln makes. Lincoln's speech is meant to persuade me to support his argument.

Speeches often contain examples to connect ideas. Lincoln uses examples to argue that boundaries are imaginary lines that are easily crossed and that the idea of dividing the land between free and slave states is wrong.

Notice the words Lincoln chose to set a tone of warning to the seceding states: *"I should expect no treaty stipulation ever made."* A treaty is a peaceful agreement.

region sloping west from the Rocky Mountains to the Pacific being the deepest, and also the richest, in undeveloped resources. In the production of provisions, grains, grasses, and all which proceed from them, this great interior region is naturally one of the most important in the world. Ascertain from the statistics the small proportion of the region which has been brought into cultivation and we shall be overwhelmed with the magnitude of the prospect presented. And yet this region has no sea-coast, touches no ocean anywhere. As part of one nation, its people now find, and may for ever find, their way to Europe by New York, to South America and Africa by New Orleans, and to Asia by San Francisco. But separate our common country into two nations, as designed by the present rebellion, and every man of this great interior region is thereby cut off from one or more of these outlets.

EXPERT READER:

I think Lincoln wants the seceding states to consider the potential of the resources found in the undeveloped interior region of the United States. If the United States is divided, the growth of this area and use of resources found there will be severely limited for them.

Lincoln warns the seceding states that the North will not participate in trade with them. Lincoln further argues that the inhabitants of the interior region will not support any lines of separation (or slavery).

And this is true, wherever a dividing or boundary line may be fixed. Place it between the now free and slave country, or place it south of Kentucky, or north of Ohio, and still the truth remains that none south of it can trade to any port or place north of it, except upon terms dictated by a government foreign to them. These outlets, east, west, and south, are indispensable to the well-being of the people inhabiting, and to inhabit, this vast interior region. Which of the three may be the best, is no proper question. All are better than either; and all of right belong to that people and their successors for ever. True to themselves, they will not ask where a line of separation shall be, but will vow rather that there shall be no such line.

Our national strife springs not from our permanent part, not from the land we inhabit, not from our national homestead. There is no possible severing of this but would multiply and not mitigate evils among us. In all its adaptations and aptitudes, it demands union and abhors separation. In fact, it would ere long force reunion, however much of blood and treasure the separation might have cost....

EXPERT READER:

Lincoln is trying to persuade the seceding states to recognize that they cannot survive separate from the Union states. He is trying to convince them now to avoid further loss of blood (life).

Fellow-citizens, we cannot escape history. We of this Congress and this Administration will be remembered in spite of ourselves. No personal significance or insignificance can spare one or another of us. The fiery trial through which we pass will light us down, in honour or dishonour, to the latest generation. We say we are for the Union. The world will not forget that we say this. We know how to save the Union. The world knows we do know how to save it.

EXPERT READER:

Lincoln compares the Civil War to a fiery trial, with the rest of the world watching to see if the Union (democracy) survives. The trial comparison alludes to right vs. wrong, slavery vs. no slavery. Lincoln again tries to convince listeners/readers to end slavery.

The words Lincoln chose, "the last, best hope of earth," convey optimism, fear, and a sense of urgency. He argues that the end of slavery and the continuation of the Union (democracy) will serve as an example to the rest of the world and is the right thing to do.

We, even we here, hold the power and bear the responsibility. In giving freedom to the slave, we assure freedom to the free, —honourable alike in what we give and what we preserve. We shall nobly save or meanly lose the last, best hope of earth. Other means may succeed; this could not fail. The way is plain, peaceful, generous, just,— a way which, if followed, the world will for ever applaud, and God must for ever bless.

The Emancipation Proclamation was an executive order issued by President Abraham Lincoln on January 1, 1863. It declared that "all persons held as slaves" within the states that were rebelling against the Union "are and henceforward shall be free."

Skill Check

Let's take a break here to let the Expert Reader summarize and analyze the ideas in this speech.

In this speech, Abraham Lincoln attempts to convince people that slavery must end and that the Union (United States) must stay united. He uses imaginary boundary lines that are easily crossed as an example to support the claim that the United States was never meant to be divided. Lincoln warns that seceding states will lose the privileges that come with being part of the Union and attempts to convince the seceding states that they cannot survive separate and apart. Although the situation is dire, Lincoln remains optimistic that slavery can be ended and that the Union can continue as a symbol of democracy for the rest of the world to aspire to.

Expert Reader: I'm satisfied with this summary. I have thought about the speech carefully, I've reread some sections to check my under-standing against text evidence, and I have used key ideas to support my summary. I'm ready to challenge my thinking by answering some multiple-choice and constructed response questions.

Mini Assessment

(Notice that in some cases, more than one answer might be consid-ered correct. It is important to use evidence to build a case for the best answer. Carefully reviewing evidence by returning to the passage will be helpful. Gauging which response is best supported through the evi-dence is critical.)

1. In paragraph four, how does Lincoln try to persuade the reader that despite the differences between the slave and free states, the Union must remain whole?

a) By explaining how the conflict can be ended.

b) By discussing the differences between the land that the slave states and free states inhabit.

c) By comparing the blood (lives) lost to the amount of money the war has cost each side.

d) By arguing that the separation of the slave states from the free states would only cause more harm to both sides.

2. In paragraph five, how does Lincoln help the reader understand the severity of the conflict between the slave and free states?

    a) By naming the Congress and administration as the cause of the situation.

    b) By comparing the conflict here to conflicts elsewhere in the world.

    c) By comparing the conflict to a fiery trial, with the verdict affecting every generation that follows.

    d) By discussing the personal significance of the conflict.

3. In the final paragraph, how does Lincoln establish the idea that the fate of democracy lies in the hands of the United States?

    a) By arguing that by freeing the slave, we set a standard to be followed by the world.

    b) By describing what freedom is.

    c) By revealing how to end the conflict between the states.

    d) By explaining that he has the ultimate responsibility for upholding democracy.

Check your answers. Were you correct?

1. d) is the best answer. Lincoln is trying to convince the reader that no one will be better off if the "homestead is severed" or separated as it will only "mitigate the evils among us." He argues that even if states were to be separated, *ere long* they would be long to be reunited.

2. c) is the best answer. Lincoln purposefully compares the conflict to fiery trial with a high-stakes verdict. He reinforces the severity of the situation when he argues that the "verdict" will affect the freedom of people living in the United States in every generation that follows.

3. a) is the best answer. Lincoln argues that the world looks to the United States to set the standard for freedom when he says "we assure freedom to the free-honourable alike in what we give and what we preserve."

Expert Reader: I'm satisfied with my responses. In all cases, I returned to the text to check against evidence. Sometimes the evidence was right there—explicitly stated or apparent. Other times, I had to dig a little deeper and use clues and inferences. In either case, my answers square with the evidence. Now I feel I'm ready to try a constructed response question.

Question: Explain how Lincoln uses the "great interior region" of the United States to convince the slave states to further reconsider their secession plans. Use at least two details from the passage to support your answer.

Possible Response: Lincoln describes the great interior region of the United States as a region with endless possibilities, to which the seceding states would not have access to. The vastness of the region and the great natural resources found there made it very desirable and as Lincoln described it "one of the naturally most important regions in the world." He argues that the statistics from the small proportion of the region that has been brought into cultivation are overwhelming with the magnitude of the prospect presented. Lincoln further suggests that people living in the interior region, either presently or in the future, will not be satisfied in observing lines of separation and will "vow that there shall be no such line." This would lead one to believe that the seceding states might have a constant battle on their hands with not only the northern states, but the states that will eventually be formed in the interior region as well.

Conclusion

How well do you feel you've grasped the Expert Reader's use of the tips and tricks for analyzing ideas, events, and individuals in informational text? Decide if you're ready to move on to the guided practice in the next chapter or if you would like to take another pass through the Expert Reader's model.

CHAPTER 5

ANALYZING IDEAS, EVENTS, AND INDIVIDUALS IN INFORMATIONAL TEXT: GUIDED PRACTICE

Now it's time for you to apply the tips and tricks during your close reading of a passage. The practice prompt icons will guide you. Check to see if your responses to the prompts match the responses provided.

An Excerpt from: Inaugural Address of Franklin Delano Roosevelt
Washington, D.C., March 4, 1933

(In November of 1932, Franklin Delano Roosevelt is elected the thirty-second president of the United States in a landslide victory over Herbert Hoover. The United States is in the middle of the Great Depression. Millions of people are unemployed, and the banking industry is failing.)

📺 GUIDED PRACTICE PROMPT:

What jump-start clues do you notice? Possible response: "Inaugural" tells me that it is President Roosevelt's first speech as president. Speeches are persuasive, so he will likely be trying to convince me of the validity of an idea(s).

What are you thinking? Possible response: It sounds like the country has some big problems. I would guess that Roosevelt will try to reassure people and give ideas for solutions.

With the nation in the middle of the Great Depression, Franklin Delano Roosevelt gave his inaugural speech, which was broadcast nationwide on several radio networks and heard by tens of millions of people.

This is a day of national consecration, and I am certain that on this day my fellow Americans expect that on my induction into the Presidency I will address them with a candor and a decision which the present situation of our people impels. This is preeminently the time to speak the truth, the whole truth, frankly and boldly. Nor need we shrink from honestly facing conditions in our country today. This great Nation will endure as it has endured, will revive and will prosper. So, first of all, let me assert my firm belief that the only thing we have to fear is fear itself—nameless, unreasoning, unjustified terror which paralyzes needed efforts to convert retreat into advance. In every dark hour of our national life a leadership of frankness and of vigor has met with that understanding and support of the people themselves which is essential to victory. And I am convinced that you will again give that support to leadership in these critical days.

In such a spirit on my part and on yours we face our common difficulties. They concern, thank God, only material things. Values have shrunk to fantastic levels; taxes have risen; our ability to pay has fallen; government of all kinds is faced by serious curtailment of income; the means of exchange are frozen in the currents of trade; the withered leaves of industrial enterprise lie on every side; farmers find no markets for their produce; and the savings

GUIDED PRACTICE PROMPT:

How can knowledge of genre and text structure help you check understanding? Possible response: Speeches persuade and give points leading to a one-sided conclusion. Roosevelt is trying to persuade people that he won't lead them astray. His position is "We will endure (get through this)." Next, he'll most likely give his plan.

GUIDED PRACTICE PROMPT:

Are you noticing the tone of the text? Possible response: I'm looking at the words used to reassure, like "nothing to fear." He's saying "We're all in this together. If you stand with me, we'll get through."

GUIDED PRACTICE PROMPT:

What are you thinking? Possible response: OK, this still sounds really bad. How will Roosevelt convince us we'll survive this?

GUIDED PRACTICE PROMPT:

How can a breakdown of literary elements help here? Possible response: Roosevelt uses compare/contrast and cause/effect to say "we've been through worse and survived," and "in light of all that's bad now, we still have a lot going for us, like the ability to grow plenty of food."

of many years in thousands of families are gone.

More important, a host of unemployed citizens face the grim problem of existence, and an equally great number toil with little return. Only a foolish optimist can deny the dark realities of the moment.

And yet our distress comes from no failure of substance. We are stricken by no plague of locusts. Compared with the perils which our forefathers conquered because they believed and were not afraid, we have still much to be thankful for. Nature still offers her bounty and human efforts have multiplied it. Plenty is at our doorstep, but a generous use of it languishes in the very sight of the supply. Primarily this is because the rulers of the exchange of mankind's goods have failed, through their own stubbornness and their own incompetence, have admitted their failure and have abdicated. Practices of the unscrupulous money changers stand indicted in the court of public opinion, rejected by the hearts and minds of men.

True they have tried, but their efforts have been cast in the pattern of an outworn tradition. Faced by failure of credit they have proposed only the lending of more money. Stripped of the lure of profit by which to induce our people to follow their false leadership, they have resorted to exhortations, pleading tearfully for restored confidence. They only know the rules of a generation of self-seekers. They have no vision, and when there is no vision the people perish.

Yes, the money changers have fled from their high seats in the temple of our civilization. We may now restore that temple to the ancient truths. The measure of that restoration lies in the extent to which we apply social values more noble than mere monetary profit.

Happiness lies not in the mere possession of money; it lies in the joy of achievement, in the thrill of creative effort. The joy, the moral stimulation of work no longer must be forgotten in the mad chase of evanescent profits. These dark days, my friends, will be worth all they cost us if they teach us that our true destiny is not to be ministered unto but to minister to ourselves—to our fellow men.

GUIDED PRACTICE PROMPT:

Are you noticing the tone of the text? Possible response: I'm noticing the words Roosevelt specifically chose. He basically compared bankers to thieves. It sounds like he blamed them for a lot of the problems.

What are you thinking? Possible response: I think Roosevelt meant that money isn't everything and that we should be happy with our achievements for the sake of achieving and helping each other.

Recognition of that falsity of material wealth as the standard of success goes hand in hand with the abandonment of the false belief that public office and high political position are to be valued only by the standards of pride of place and personal profit; and there must be an end to a conduct in banking and in business which too often has given to a sacred trust the likeness of callous and selfish wrongdoing. Small wonder that confidence languishes, for it thrives only on honesty, on honor, on the sacredness of obligations, on faithful protection, and on unselfish performance; without them it cannot live.

GUIDED PRACTICE PROMPT:

How can a breakdown of literary elements help here? Possible response: I'm noticing the word choice and the categorization that connects honesty, truth, unselfishness, and confidence as Roosevelt continued to make his point that we'll come out of this hard time better than we started.

Restoration calls, however, not for changes in ethics alone. This Nation is asking for action, and action now.

Our greatest primary task is to put people to work. This is no unsolvable problem if we face it wisely and courageously. It can be accomplished in part by direct recruiting by the Government itself, treating the task as we would treat the emergency of a war, but at the same time, through this employment, accomplishing greatly needed projects to stimulate and reorganize the use of our great natural resources.

GUIDED PRACTICE PROMPT:

What are you thinking? Possible response: After reading, I'm thinking this was probably a fairly powerful speech. It's persuasive, and Roosevelt gave people hope that with hard work and improved ethics, life will get better.

Quick Check Self-Evaluation for Analyzing Ideas, Events, and Individuals

At this point, you should be able to summarize this speech and think about its intended purpose. Refer to page 11 to review the criteria. What is the strongest evidence to support the central idea? Go ahead and try it! Talk through your answer, or jot it down on a separate piece of paper. (See the Expert Reader's summary.)

Once you're satisfied and have checked your responses, challenge your thinking and answer the multiple-choice and constructed response questions that follow.

Expert Reader's summary: *This speech was given during a time of great economic hardship for the United States. President Roosevelt talked frankly and honestly with the American people about the poor financial condition of the country. He also reminded people that although they may have lost material items, our ancestors went through far worse to make a better life for their children. He persuaded people that by standing together as one and* *relying upon honesty, honor, and hard work, the country can move past this time of hardship.*

(Your summary may be somewhat different from the Expert Reader's, and that's OK, as long as it holds up under scrutiny and squares with the supporting textual evidence.)

Mini Assessment

(Again, be aware that it is important to use evidence to build a case for the best answer. Remember to carefully review evidence by returning to the passage to gauge which response is best supported.)

1. How did President Roosevelt illustrate his belief that the people of the United States have the means to help themselves get through these difficult times?

a) By describing his plan for recovery.
b) By explaining that in order to move forward and out of this crisis, people will need to overcome their fear that all is lost.
c) By revealing that he will speak truthfully.
d) By arguing that it's not the government's fault.

2. How did President Roosevelt make a connection between happiness and work?

a) By describing how the savings of many families have been lost.
b) By stating that it is the government's job to create jobs for people.
c) By arguing that hard work and creativity bring joy.
d) By telling that there is no problem too large that can't be solved.

3. How did President Roosevelt introduce the key idea of the importance of the government helping to create jobs that put people back to work?

When constructing a summary, it is critical to think about the author's intended purpose, as well as which evidence from the text best supports the author's intent.

a) He compared the unemployment problem to the way we would treat the occurrence of a war.

b) He listed the problems that the unemployed are facing.

c) He told a story about money changers who fled from their high seats.

d) He listed the jobs that people will be working on.

Check your answers. Were you correct?

1 b) is the best answer. Roosevelt stated "that the only thing we have to fear is fear itself" and further explained when people are fearful, they are frequently paralyzed, which makes them unable to move forward. Therefore, they must overcome their fears to get through these difficult times.

2 c) is the best answer. Roosevelt argued that "happiness lies not in the mere possession of money; it lies in the joy of achievement, in the thrill of creative effort", which makes c) the best answer.

3 a) is the best answer. Roosevelt stated that the government's primary task is to put people to work and compared the importance of this task to other important emergencies that the United States might encounter, such as wars.

What do you think so far? Is your understanding and analysis of the passage taking shape? Did you return to the passage and find evidence to support your responses? Did your answers square with the evidence? Are you comfortable discussing or writing a response to the following constructed response question? Again, either talk through your answer or jot it down on a separate piece of paper and then check your response against the possible response.

Authors of informational text have a point to make about a topic. They frequently want to change readers' thinking in some way or add to their understanding.

Question: Explain how President Roosevelt connected the loss of savings of thousands of families to the failure of the banking system. Use at least two details from the passage to support your answer.

Possible response: President Roosevelt blamed the incompetence of the banking system for the financial losses sustained by thousands of people. In fact, he stated that the people in charge of banking have "admitted their failure and have abdicated," or run away from their responsibilities. He further stated that these same people have "pleaded tearfully for restored confidence," but that people do not trust them any longer because they only know the "rules of a generation of self-seekers," meaning their interest is in helping themselves versus helping the people who entrusted their savings to them.

Conclusion

How well have you grasped the tips and tricks for analyzing how and why individuals, events, and ideas develop and interact over the course of a text? Based on your performance and self-evaluations, decide if you've mastered the skills or if you would like to take another pass through this guided practice. Congratulations if you're ready to move on!

A New Expert Reader!

Now that you've mastered how to use the tips and tricks for analyzing how and why individuals, events, and ideas develop and interact over the course of a text, you're on your way to becoming an Expert Reader! Continue to practice with different types of literature and informational texts. You'll see that your attempts to grapple with classroom and assigned texts are far easier now.

GLOSSARY

ADAPTATION A passage of writing that is altered (shortened or revised) so that it can be presented in another form.

ANALYZE To carefully examine, inspect, and consider a text in order to fully understand it.

CENTRAL IDEA The key concept or message being expressed.

CLOSE READING The deep, analytical reading of a brief passage of text in which the reader constructs meaning based on author intention and text evidence. The close reading of a text enables readers to gain insights that exceed a cursory reading.

DISTRACTOR Anything that steers a reader away from the text evidence and weakens or misguides analysis.

EVIDENCE Information from the text that a reader uses to prove a position, conclusion, inference, or big idea.

EXPERT An individual who is particularly skilled or knowledgeable about a subject and therefore held in high regard.

FIX-UP STRATEGY A common technique used when meaning is lost.

GENRE A system used to classify kinds or writing.

INFERENCE A conclusion that a reader draws about something by using information that is available.

INFORMATIONAL TEXT A type of nonfiction text, such as articles, essays, opinion pieces, memoirs, and historical, scientific, technical, or economic accounts that are written to give facts or inform about a topic.

LITERARY ELEMENTS The component parts found in a whole work of literature.

LITERATURE Imaginary stories, such as mysteries, myths, creation stories, science fiction, allegories, and other genres that include elements such as characters, problems or conflicts, setting, plot with events or episodes, and problem resolution.

PERSUASIVE TEXT Nonfiction text intended to convince the reader of the validity of a set of ideas.

POINT OF VIEW The perspective, or position, from which the story is told.

SUBHEADING A phrase in larger font or bold-faced print that provides information on the topic of a section of text.

SUMMARY A short account of a text that gives the main points but not all the details.

TEXT FEATURES The variety of tools used to organize text and give readers more information about the text.

TEXT STRUCTURE The way in which information is organized within a written text.

TONE The writer's communication of an overall feeling or attitude about a book's subject, content, or topic.

FOR MORE INFORMATION

Council of Chief State School Officers
One Massachusetts Avenue, NW Suite 700
Washington, DC 20001-1431
(202) 336-7000
Website: http://www.ccsso.org
The Common Core State Standards Initiative is a state-led effort coor-
dinated by the National Governors Association Center for Best
Practices (NGA Center) and the Council of Chief State School
Officers (CCSSO). The standards provide a clear and consistent
framework to prepare students for college and the workforce.

National Governors Association
Hall of the States
444 North Capitol Street, Suite 267
Washington, DC 20001-1512
(202) 624-5300
Website: http://www.nga.org

National Parent Teacher Association
12250 North Pitt Street
Alexandria, VA 22314
(703) 518-1200
Website: http://www.pta.org
National PTA enthusiastically supports the adoption and implementation by all states of the Common Core State Standards. The
standards form a solid foundation for high quality education.

New York State Education Department
89 Washington Avenue
Albany, NY 12234

(518) 474-3852

Website: http://www.engageny.org

EngageNY.org was developed and is maintained by the New York State Education Department. This is the official website for current materials and resources related to the implementation of the New York State P–12 Common Core Learning Standards (CCLS).

U.S. Department of Education

Department of Education Building

400 Maryland Avenue SW

Washington, DC 20202

(800) 872-5327

Website: http://www.edu.gov

Nearly every state now has adopted the Common Core State Standards. The federal government has supported this state-led effort by helping to ensure that higher standards are being implemented for all students and that educators are being supported in transitioning to new standards.

Websites

Due to the changing nature of Internet links, Rosen Publishing has developed an online list of websites related to the subject of this book. This site is updated regularly. Please use this link to access the list:

http://www.rosenlinks.com/Ideas

BIBLIOGRAPHY

Beers, Kylene, and Robert E. Probst. *Notice & Note: Strategies for Close Reading*. Heinemann: Portsmouth, NH, 2013

Calkins, Lucy, Mary Ehrenworth, and Christopher Lehman. *Pathways to the Common Core: Accelerating Achievement*. Portsmouth, NH: Heinemann, 2012.

Cather, Willa. *My Antonia*. First published in 1918. (Adaptation based on the original work)

Irene C. Fountas, and Gay Su Pinnell. *Genre Study: Teaching with Fiction and Nonfiction Books*. Heinemann: Portsmouth, NH, 2012

Janeczko, Paul B. *Reading Poetry in the Middle Grades: 20 Poems and Activities That Meet the Common Core Standards and Cultivate a Passion for Poetry*. Portsmouth, NH: Heinemann, 2011.

Lincoln, Abraham (1862, October). *Annual Message to Congress*. Speech Presented at Washington, D.C.

London, Jack. *Call of the Wild*. First published in 1903. (Adaptation based on the original work)

McLaughlin, Maureen. *The Common Core: Teaching K–5 Students to Meet the Reading Standards*. Newark, DE: International Reading Association, 2012.

Roosevelt, Franklin Delano (1933, March). *Inaugural Address*. Speech Presented at Washington, D.C.

INDEX

About the Authors

Sandra K. Athans is a National Board Certified practicing classroom teacher with fifteen years of experience teaching reading and writing at the elementary level. She is the author of several teacher-practitioner books on literacy, including *Quality Comprehension* and *Fun-tastic Activities for Differentiating Comprehension Instruction*, both published by the International Reading Association. Athans has presented her research at the International Reading Association, the National Council of Teachers of English Conferences, and at the New York State Reading Association Conferences. Her contributions have appeared in well-known literacy works, including *The Literacy Leadership Handbook* and *Strategic Writing Mini-Lessons*. She is also a children's book writer and specializes in high-interest, photo-informational books published with Millbrook Press, a Division of Lerner Publishing Group.

Athans earned a B.A. in English from the University of Michigan, an M.A. in elementary education from Manhattanville College, and an M.S. in literacy from Le Moyne College. She is also certified to teach secondary english. In addition to teaching in the classroom, she is an adjunct professor at Le Moyne College and provides instruction in graduate-level literacy classes. This spring she was named Outstanding Elementary Social Studies Educator by the Central New York Council for the Social Studies. She serves on various ELA leadership networks and collaborates with educators nationwide to address the challenges of the Common Core standards. The Tips and Tricks series is among several Common Core resources she has authored for Rosen Publishing.

Robin W. Parente is a practicing reading specialist and classroom teacher with over fifteen years of experience teaching reading and writing at the elementary level. She also serves as the Elementary ELA

Coordinator for a medium-sized district in central New York, working with classroom teachers to implement best literacy practices in the classroom. Parente earned a B.S. in elementary education and an M.S. in education/literacy from the State University of New York, Oswego. She is a certified reading specialist (PK–12) and elementary classroom teacher and has served on various ELA leadership networks to collaborate with educators to address the challenges of the Common Core standards. The Tips and Tricks series is among several Common Core resources she has authored for Rosen Publishing.

Photo Credits

Cover © iStockphoto.com/xua; pp. 4–5 Christopher Futcher/Vetta/Getty Images; p. 8 Estudi M6/iStock/Thinkstock; p. 13 lightpoet/Shutterstock.com; p. 15 Photo Inc./Photo Researchers/Getty Images; p. 21 Michael S. Lewis/National Geographic Image Collection/Getty Images; p. 32 Rita Kochmarjova/Shutterstock.com; p. 35 Stock Montage/Archive Photos/Getty Images; p. 40 George Eastman House/Archive Photos /Getty Images; p. 46 FPG/Archive Photos/Getty Images; p. 52 REB Images/Blend Images/Getty Images; p. 54 © iStockphoto.com/RapidEye; icons © iStockphoto/sodafish, © iStockphoto.com/kimberywood, © iStockphoto/Aaltazar.

Designer: Nicole Russo; Editor: Bethany Bryan; Photo Researcher: Karen Huang